CW01512126

the tuskegee deception

A Short Account of the Infamous Syphilis Study

william webb

contents

introduction

background and overview of the tuskegee syphilis study

Imagine a time when medical research was far from the ethical and regulated field it is today—a time when human lives were treated as mere tools for scientific discovery, with little regard for their well-being. This might sound like a plot from a dystopian novel, but it was a reality for hundreds of African American men who were unknowingly part of one of the most infamous medical research studies in history: the Tuskegee Syphilis Study.

So, what was the Tuskegee Syphilis Study all about? Well, it was a 40-year-long experiment conducted by the United States Public Health Service (USPHS) in collaboration with the Tuskegee Institute, a historically black college in Alabama. The study began in 1932 and involved around 600 African American men—399 with syphilis and 201 without the disease, who served as the control group. The purpose of the study was to observe the natural progression of untreated syphilis in African American men, under the guise of providing them with free healthcare.

Now, you might be wondering, "Why would they not treat these men for such a dangerous disease?" That's where the dark side of this study lies. The researchers had no intention of treating the participants, even after penicillin was discovered as a cure for syphilis in the 1940s. The men were never informed about their syphilis diagnosis, nor were they told the true nature of the study. Instead, they were deceived into believing they were receiving medical care for "bad blood," a term used to describe various ailments.

As the years went by, many of these men suffered and died from syphilis and its complications, while the researchers continued to observe the effects of the disease on their bodies. Their families were also affected, as spouses and children were at risk of contracting the disease.

The study continued in secret until 1972 when a whistleblower named Peter Buxtun exposed the horrifying truth behind it. Public outrage ensued, and the study was finally terminated. The aftermath of this revelation led to a series of investigations, legal actions, and eventually, the development of modern medical research ethics.

Now that we've covered the basics of the Tuskegee Syphilis Study, let's dive deeper into the historical context, the ethical violations, and the lasting legacy of this shocking experiment that forever changed the landscape of medical research.

significance of the study in the history of medical ethics

When we think about the Tuskegee Syphilis Study, it's impossible not to feel a mix of shock, anger, and disbelief. But despite its dark nature, the study served as a turning point in medical ethics, leading to significant changes in the way researchers conduct experiments and treat human subjects.

Before the Tuskegee study was exposed, there were far fewer regulations protecting the rights and well-being of research participants. Believe it or not, informed consent wasn't always a standard practice, and researchers often prioritized their findings over the welfare of their subjects. But after the horrifying truth about the Tuskegee study came to light, people began to question the ethics of medical research, and the scientific community was forced to take a hard look at its practices.

One of the most significant outcomes of the Tuskegee study was the establishment of the National Commission for the Protection of Human Subjects of Biomedical and Behavioral Research in 1974. The commission was tasked with evaluating research ethics and creating guidelines for the protection of human subjects. The result? The Belmont Report, published in 1979, which laid out the ethical principles and guidelines for conducting research on humans. This report has since become the cornerstone of modern medical ethics, emphasizing respect for persons, beneficence, and justice.

The Belmont Report also led to the creation of Institutional Review Boards (IRBs). These boards are responsible for reviewing and approving research proposals, ensuring that they comply with ethical guidelines and prioritize the safety and well-being of participants. Today, it's hard to imagine a world without IRBs, but before the Tuskegee study, their existence wasn't even a consideration.

Another significant impact of the study was a greater emphasis on informed consent. In the wake of the Tuskegee scandal, it became clear that participants must be fully informed about the nature of a study, its potential risks, and their right to withdraw at any time. This crucial shift in focus helps protect the rights and autonomy of research subjects, ensuring that they are treated with the dignity and respect they deserve.

It's undeniable that the Tuskegee Syphilis Study was a dark chapter in the history of medical research. But, in a way, it served as a catalyst for change. The outrage and public scrutiny that followed forced researchers to reevaluate their practices and embrace a more ethical approach. While we can never undo the harm caused by the Tuskegee study, we can take solace in the fact that its legacy has led to better protections and a more ethical framework for medical research today.

purpose of the book

The Tuskegee Syphilis Study is a story that needs to be told—not just as a cautionary tale, but as a reminder of the importance of ethics, compassion, and humanity in medical research. The purpose of this book is to provide an in-depth exploration of the study, its historical context, and its lasting impact on the world of medicine and beyond.

By examining the origins, development, and eventual unraveling of the study, we hope to shed light on the circumstances that allowed such a gross violation of human rights to occur. Through this exploration, we aim to foster a deeper understanding of how systemic racism, unchecked scientific ambition, and a lack of oversight can lead to tragic consequences.

This book also intends to honor the memory of the victims of the Tuskegee Syphilis Study—the men who suffered needlessly and the families who bore the burden of the study's consequences. By acknowledging their pain and giving voice to their stories, we can ensure that their experiences are not forgotten and serve as a constant reminder of the importance of ethical conduct in medical research.

Moreover, we want to highlight the lasting legacy of the Tuskegee study in shaping modern medical ethics. By examining the changes it inspired and the safeguards that were put in place following its exposure, we aim to emphasize the significance of ethical considerations in scientific research and the ongoing need for vigilance in maintaining these standards.

Finally, this book serves as a call to action—a reminder that we must continue to work towards racial equality in healthcare and strive to rebuild trust between marginalized communities and the medical establishment. By learning from the past and acknowledging the injustices that have been perpetrated, we can work together to create a brighter, more equitable future for all.

In essence, this book is a journey through a dark chapter in medical history, a tribute to the victims, and an exploration of the lessons learned from the Tuskegee Syphilis Study. Through this journey, we hope to inspire readers to reflect on the importance of ethics, compassion, and social justice in the world of medicine and beyond.

1 /
historical context

early 20th century america

TO TRULY UNDERSTAND the Tuskegee Syphilis Study, we need to travel back in time and take a look at the social landscape of early 20th century America. Picture a nation that was rapidly evolving, yet still grappling with deep-rooted racial segregation and discrimination. This was an era marked by the "Jim Crow" laws, which enforced racial segregation in the Southern United States and perpetuated inequality between white Americans and African Americans.

During this time, African Americans faced significant challenges in accessing basic resources, including education and healthcare. Segregated hospitals and medical facilities were the norm, and there was a severe shortage of African American doctors and nurses. As a result, many African Americans had limited access to quality medical care, making them more vulnerable to diseases and health issues.

In addition to these structural barriers, there was a widespread mistrust of the medical establishment among African Americans—and for good reason. The history of medical experimentation on African Americans without their consent dates back to the days of slavery. This history, coupled with rampant racism within the medical community, further deepened the divide between African Americans and healthcare providers.

Amidst this backdrop of racial segregation and inequality, syphilis emerged as a significant public health concern in the United States. The disease was particularly prevalent among African American communities, where limited access to healthcare and mistrust of the medical establishment made it difficult to address the growing epidemic.

It's important to understand this historical context, as it provides insight into the circumstances that allowed the Tuskegee Syphilis Study to take place. The racial disparities in healthcare and the growing urgency to address the syphilis epidemic set the stage for a research study that ultimately violated the trust and rights of its participants. As we delve deeper into the origins and development of the Tuskegee study, keep this social landscape in mind—it's a crucial piece of the puzzle in understanding how such a tragedy could have occurred.

the development of syphilis research

While syphilis was a growing concern in the United States, researchers were also trying to understand the disease and find effective treatments. Let's take a closer look at the development of syphilis research during this time and how it contributed to the launch of the Tuskegee Syphilis Study.

The Oslo Study

Before Tuskegee, there was the Oslo Study. Conducted in Norway between 1891 and 1910, the Oslo Study was a retrospective examination of patients with untreated syphilis. Unlike the Tuskegee study, the Oslo study didn't involve withholding treatment; it simply observed the natural course of the disease in patients who had never received treatment. The findings from the Oslo study provided valuable insights into the progression of syphilis and its various stages, but it also raised questions about the long-term effects of the disease on different populations.

The Emergence of the Syphilis Epidemic in the United States

As syphilis rates continued to rise in the United States, the USPHS began to take notice. They were particularly concerned about the high rates of infection among African Americans and sought to better understand the impact of the disease on this population. This interest, combined with the findings from the Oslo study, ultimately laid the groundwork for the Tuskegee Syphilis Study.

The USPHS believed that studying the progression of untreated syphilis in African Americans could help them develop targeted public health interventions and better address the syphilis epidemic. However, the decision to withhold treatment and deceive the study participants was a grave ethical misstep—one that would have devastating consequences for the men involved and their families.

Now that we've explored the historical context of early 20th century America and the development of syphilis research, we're ready to dive into the origins and development of the Tuskegee Syphilis Study itself. As we examine the planning, recruitment, and execution of this infamous study, we'll see how the convergence of scientific ambition, systemic racism, and a lack of ethical oversight led to one of the darkest chapters in medical history.

2 /
the tuskegee syphilis study: origins and development

planning and initiation

NOW THAT WE'VE set the stage, let's dive into the planning and initiation of the Tuskegee Syphilis Study. How did the idea come to life, and who were the key players involved in launching this ill-fated research project?

Collaboration between the United States Public Health Service (USPHS) and Tuskegee Institute

The partnership between the USPHS and the Tuskegee Institute was a critical component in the development of the study. The USPHS, a federal agency focused on public health, was keen on understanding the impact of syphilis on the African American population. The Tuskegee Institute, a prominent historically black college in Alabama, seemed like the perfect partner for this endeavor. The institute was well-respected within the African American community and had strong ties to local medical professionals, which would prove invaluable in recruiting participants and gaining the community's trust.

Study Objectives and Research Questions

The main objective of the Tuskegee Syphilis Study was to observe the natural progression of untreated syphilis in African American men. Researchers wanted to know if the disease manifested differently in African Americans compared to other populations, and if there were any unique long-term effects. Additionally, they hoped to gather data on the impact of syphilis on the cardiovascular and neurological systems.

While these research questions may have seemed reasonable, the study's underlying assumption—that African Americans with syphilis would go untreated anyway—reflected the pervasive racism of the time. This assumption disregarded the participants' right to treatment and ultimately led to a study design that would prioritize scientific curiosity over human well-being.

As we continue to explore the Tuskegee Syphilis Study, we'll examine the recruitment process, the study design, and the ethical violations that took place throughout the experiment. Keep in mind the context we've discussed thus far, as it provides a lens through which we can better understand the decisions made by the researchers and the tragic consequences that followed.

recruitment and study design

With the stage set and the objectives outlined, the Tuskegee Syphilis Study moved into the recruitment and study design phases. This section will delve into the strategies used to recruit participants, the study design itself, and the role of deception in the study's execution.

Recruitment of Participants

The researchers faced the challenge of recruiting African American men with syphilis for the study. To gain the trust of potential participants, they collaborated with local African American doctors, nurses, and community leaders, who played a crucial role in persuading men to enroll in the study. Many of the recruits were poor sharecroppers with limited access to healthcare, which made the prospect of free medical care particularly enticing.

The researchers also targeted churches and community centers, using these trusted institutions to spread the word about the study. By tapping into the social networks of the African American community, they were able to recruit around 600 men—399 with syphilis and 201 without the disease, who served as the control group.

The Deception

One of the most disturbing aspects of the Tuskegee Syphilis Study was the use of deception. The researchers never informed the participants about their syphilis diagnosis, nor did they explain the true nature of the study. Instead, the men were led to believe they were receiving treatment for "bad blood"—a vague term used to describe various ailments.

Throughout the study, participants were given placebo treatments, such as aspirin and vitamins, to maintain the illusion of medical care. They were also subjected to invasive and painful medical procedures, such as spinal taps, which were presented as "therapeutic" but were actually conducted for research purposes.

The Study Design

The study was designed as a long-term observational study, with the researchers closely monitoring the health of the participants over time. The goal was to document the progression of untreated syphilis, with a particular focus on the impact of the disease on the cardiovascular and neurological systems.

As the years went by, the researchers diligently

collected data on the participants' health, even as their conditions deteriorated. The study continued, despite the availability of penicillin as a cure for syphilis in the 1940s. The researchers' decision to withhold this life-saving treatment from the participants was a flagrant ethical violation that would ultimately lead to the study's infamy.

In the following sections, we'll explore the study's unraveling and exposure, the public response, and the lasting impact of the Tuskegee Syphilis Study on medical research ethics. As we navigate this dark chapter in history, it's important to remember the context and motivations that led to the study's inception and the disturbing choices made by those involved.

study design and procedures

The Tuskegee Syphilis Study was designed as a long-term observational study, with the primary goal of understanding the natural progression of untreated syphilis in African American men. In this section, we'll take a closer look at the study's design and procedures, shedding light on how the researchers conducted the study and the methods they employed.

Recruitment of Participants

The researchers targeted African American men in Macon County, Alabama, due to its high syphilis prevalence. They collaborated with local healthcare providers, who played a key role in recruiting participants. Many of the men were sharecroppers, with limited access to healthcare and low socioeconomic status. In total, 600 men were enrolled, with 399 having syphilis and 201 serving as a control group without the disease.

The Promise of Treatment

The participants were misled to believe they were receiving treatment for "bad blood," a term commonly used to describe a variety of health issues, including syphilis. In reality, the researchers provided only minimal treatment, such as aspirin and iron supplements, which had no curative effect on syphilis. The men were also offered free medical exams, meals, and burial insurance as incentives to participate.

Observation and Data Collection

Throughout the study, the researchers periodically examined the participants, collecting blood samples, performing spinal taps, and monitoring their health. The goal was to document the progression of syphilis and its complications, including cardiovascular issues and neurological damage. However, the men were not informed about their syphilis diagnosis or the true purpose of these examinations.

Withholding Effective Treatment

When penicillin emerged as the standard treatment for syphilis in the 1940s, the researchers chose not to provide it to the participants, despite its proven efficacy. Instead, they continued to observe the men as their health deteriorated, even going so far as to prevent them from accessing treatment through other sources.

The Study's Duration

The Tuskegee Syphilis Study was initially intended to last six months but ultimately continued for 40 years, from 1932 to 1972. Despite multiple opportunities to reconsider the study's ethics, the researchers persisted in their pursuit of data on untreated syphilis, resulting in unnecessary suffering and death for many participants.

The study's design and procedures reveal a disturbing pattern of deception, exploitation, and disregard for the well-being of its participants. Understanding these elements is essential to grasping the full extent of the ethical violations that occurred and recognizing the need for continued vigilance in medical research ethics.

3 /
ethical violations

informed consent

IN THE WAKE of the Tuskegee Syphilis Study, one of the most significant ethical issues that came to the forefront was the concept of informed consent. The lack of informed consent in the study was a glaring violation of the participants' rights, and it has since become a cornerstone of modern medical ethics. Let's dive into what informed consent means and why it's so crucial in research involving human subjects.

The Principles of Informed Consent

Informed consent is a process through which potential research participants are provided with all the relevant information about a study, allowing them to make an educated decision about whether to participate. This process is built on several key principles:

- Respect for autonomy: Researchers must respect the autonomy and decision-making capabilities of potential participants. This means giving them the freedom to decide whether to participate without coercion or manipulation.
- Disclosure of information: Researchers are obligated to provide participants with comprehensive information about the study, including its purpose, the procedures involved, potential risks and benefits, and any alternative treatments that may be available.
- Comprehension: Researchers must ensure that participants fully understand the information provided to them. This may involve using clear, non-technical language and checking for understanding before proceeding.
- Voluntariness: Participation in research must be entirely voluntary. Participants should feel free to decline or withdraw from a study at any time, without fear of repercussions or penalties.

The Importance of Informed Consent

Informed consent is crucial for protecting the rights and well-being of research participants. It empowers individuals to make informed decisions about their own bodies and health, ensuring that they are treated with dignity and respect.

Moreover, informed consent helps to build trust between researchers and participants, fostering a positive relationship that is conducive to successful research outcomes. It also serves as a safeguard against potential abuses of power and unethical practices, helping to prevent tragedies like the Tuskegee Syphilis Study from happening again.

The Legacy of the Tuskegee Syphilis Study in Informed Consent

The Tuskegee Syphilis Study served as a wake-up call for the medical community, highlighting the urgent need for stricter ethical guidelines and oversight in research involving human subjects. Following the study's exposure, the government implemented new regulations and guidelines to ensure the protection of research participants, with informed consent becoming a fundamental requirement in human research.

In today's research landscape, informed consent is a non-negotiable element of ethical research practice. The Tuskegee Syphilis Study stands as a stark reminder of the consequences of disregarding the rights and dignity of research participants, and the importance of maintaining the highest ethical standards in medical research.

withholding treatment

One of the most shocking aspects of the Tuskegee Syphilis Study was the researchers' decision to withhold treatment from the participants, even when an effective cure became available. This aspect of the study raises critical questions about the ethical responsibilities of researchers and the importance of prioritizing the well-being of participants. Let's delve into the issue of withholding treatment and the lessons we can learn from this disturbing element of the study.

The Arrival of Penicillin

In the 1940s, penicillin emerged as a highly effective treatment for syphilis. As the miracle drug became more widely available, it had the potential to save countless lives and put an end to the suffering of those afflicted with the disease. However, in the case of the Tuskegee Syphilis Study, the researchers chose not to administer penicillin to the participants, despite knowing that it could cure their illness.

Ethical Implications of Withholding Treatment

The decision to withhold treatment from the study participants was a clear ethical violation. It demonstrated a blatant disregard for the participants' health and well-being, prioritizing the study's objectives over the lives of the men involved. This decision not only caused unnecessary suffering for the participants but also had long-lasting consequences for their families and communities.

Lessons Learned and the Duty to Provide Treatment

The Tuskegee Syphilis Study serves as a powerful reminder of the ethical obligation researchers have to prioritize the well-being of their participants. It highlights the importance of putting participants' health and safety first, even if doing so may impact the study's outcomes.

In the aftermath of the study, researchers and ethicists have emphasized the duty to provide treatment in clinical research settings. This includes offering the best available treatment options and ensuring that participants are not denied access to effective therapies simply because they are part of a study.

The Impact on Future Research

The tragedy of the Tuskegee Syphilis Study has had a lasting impact on the conduct of future research, particularly in terms of how researchers approach the issue of withholding treatment. Today, clinical trials must adhere to strict ethical guidelines that prioritize the well-being of participants and ensure that they receive the best possible care.

By remembering the lessons of the Tuskegee Syphilis Study, we can work to prevent similar ethical breaches from occurring in the future. The study serves as a stark reminder of the responsibility researchers have to their participants and the importance of maintaining the highest ethical standards in medical research.

the study's impact on participants and their families

The Tuskegee Syphilis Study didn't just affect the men who were directly involved; it also had lasting consequences for their families and communities. In this section, we'll explore the ripple effects of the study on the lives of those who were connected to the participants and the ongoing challenges faced by their descendants.

Health Consequences for Participants

As we know, the participants in the study were denied proper treatment for their syphilis, which led to many of them suffering from the severe health consequences of untreated syphilis. These consequences included damage to the heart, brain, nerves, and other organs, as well as an increased risk of death. The men in the study, unaware of their true diagnosis, unwittingly put their loved ones at risk.

Impact on Spouses and Children

The wives and partners of the participants in the Tuskegee Syphilis Study were also profoundly affected by the study's unethical practices. Many of these women were unknowingly exposed to syphilis through their partners and subsequently contracted the disease themselves. This, in turn, led to a risk of congenital syphilis, in which the infection is passed from mother to child during pregnancy, resulting in severe health complications or even death for the newborns.

Emotional and Psychological Effects

The deception and betrayal at the heart of the Tuskegee Syphilis Study had lasting emotional and psychological effects on the participants and their families. Learning the truth about the study and the researchers' callous disregard for their well-being left many feeling angry, hurt, and disillusioned. The lingering mistrust of the medical establishment is an understandable legacy of this tragic episode.

The Ongoing Struggle for Justice and Healing

In the years following the exposure of the Tuskegee Syphilis Study, survivors and their families sought justice and compensation for the harm they had endured. In 1974, a class-action lawsuit resulted in a $10 million settlement, which included lifetime medical benefits and burial services for the study participants and their families.

While monetary compensation can never fully make up for the suffering caused by the study, it was an important step in acknowledging the wrongs that were committed. The process of healing and reconciliation is ongoing, with efforts being made to educate future generations about the study's history and its impact on the African American community.

The Tuskegee Syphilis Study serves as a powerful reminder of the importance of ethical research practices and the need to prioritize the well-being of participants and their families. By understanding the study's devastating impact on the lives of those involved, we can work to prevent such tragedies from happening again and ensure that future research is guided by compassion and respect for human dignity.

4 /
the unraveling of the tuskegee syphilis study

whistleblowers and public exposure

THE TRUTH about the Tuskegee Syphilis Study would have remained hidden if it hadn't been for the courage and tenacity of whistleblowers who brought the unethical practices to light. In this section, we'll discuss the individuals who played a key role in exposing the study and the public response that followed.

Peter Buxtun: A Persistent Whistleblower

Peter Buxtun, a former employee of the U.S. Public Health Service (PHS), was one of the first whistleblowers to raise concerns about the Tuskegee Syphilis Study. Buxtun, who worked as a venereal disease investigator, learned about the study in 1966 and was disturbed by its unethical conduct. He reported his concerns to his superiors at the PHS, but his complaints fell on deaf ears.

Undeterred, Buxtun took his concerns to the press in 1972, providing information to Jean Heller of the Associated Press. Heller's subsequent article about the study brought the scandal to the attention of the wider public, sparking widespread outrage and demands for accountability.

The Role of the Media in Exposing the Study

Once the story broke, it didn't take long for the media to pick up on the shocking details of the Tuskegee Syphilis Study. Newspapers, magazines, and television programs across the country reported on the study's unethical practices and the suffering of its participants. The public exposure played a crucial role in bringing the study to an end and initiating the process of seeking justice for the participants and their families.

Congressional Hearings and Public Response

In response to the public outcry, Congress held hearings to investigate the Tuskegee Syphilis Study, and in 1973, a panel of experts concluded that the study was "ethically unjustified." The panel's findings led to the termination of the study and the implementation of new ethical guidelines for conducting research involving human subjects.

The public response to the exposure of the

Tuskegee Syphilis Study was a mix of shock, outrage, and disbelief. Many people were appalled by the government's role in the study and the blatant disregard for the rights and well-being of its participants. The scandal served as a wake-up call for the need to ensure that medical research is conducted ethically and with respect for human dignity.

The Legacy of Whistleblowers

The whistleblowers who exposed the Tuskegee Syphilis Study played a crucial role in bringing the scandal to light and initiating change in the field of medical research ethics. Their courage and determination to reveal the truth serve as a reminder of the importance of holding institutions accountable for their actions, even when doing so may be difficult or unpopular.

The story of the Tuskegee Syphilis Study's exposure highlights the power of individuals to make a difference and the critical role of the media in holding powerful institutions accountable. By learning from this dark chapter in history, we can work to ensure that future research is guided by ethical principles and a commitment to protecting the rights and well-being of all participants.

official investigation and hearings

The public exposure of the Tuskegee Syphilis Study led to a series of official investigations and hearings that aimed to uncover the full extent of the unethical practices and hold those responsible accountable. In this section, we'll delve into the process of these investigations, their findings, and the steps taken to address the issues they uncovered.

The Formation of the Ad Hoc Advisory Panel

In response to the public outcry, the U.S. Department of Health, Education, and Welfare (HEW) formed the Ad Hoc Advisory Panel in 1972. This panel, composed of medical experts, ethicists, and civil rights leaders, was tasked with reviewing the Tuskegee Syphilis Study and determining its ethical implications.

Findings of the Ad Hoc Advisory Panel

After a thorough investigation, the Ad Hoc Advisory Panel concluded that the Tuskegee Syphilis Study was "ethically unjustified." They determined that the study's researchers had deceived the participants and that their failure to provide them with proper treatment for syphilis was a gross violation of their rights and well-being. The panel's findings led to the termination of the study in 1973.

Congressional Hearings

Following the panel's findings, Congress held a series of hearings to further investigate the study and its implications. These hearings aimed to uncover the full extent of the ethical violations and examine the role of the government and other institutions involved in the study. During the hearings, testimony was provided by whistleblowers, participants, researchers, and other witnesses, shedding light on the study's disturbing practices.

Policy Changes and New Ethical Guidelines

The investigations and hearings surrounding the Tuskegee Syphilis Study prompted a significant shift in the ethical landscape of medical research. As a result, new policies and guidelines were implemented to ensure that human subjects were protected in future studies.

One major outcome of the hearings was the establishment of the National Commission for the Protection of Human Subjects of Biomedical and Behavioral Research in 1974. This commission was responsible for creating the Belmont Report, which outlined key ethical principles for conducting research involving human subjects. These principles, including respect for persons, beneficence, and justice, continue to guide medical research today.

A Turning Point in Medical Research Ethics

The official investigations and hearings that

followed the exposure of the Tuskegee Syphilis Study marked a turning point in the history of medical research ethics. The scandal revealed the urgent need for robust ethical guidelines and oversight to protect the rights and well-being of research participants.

The impact of the Tuskegee Syphilis Study on the field of medical research ethics cannot be overstated. The lessons learned from this tragic episode continue to inform ethical decision-making and policy development, ensuring that future research is conducted with the utmost respect for human dignity and the well-being of all participants.

legal actions and settlements

The exposure of the Tuskegee Syphilis Study led to a series of legal actions taken by the participants and their families in an effort to seek justice and compensation for the harm they had endured. In this section, we'll discuss the legal proceedings that unfolded, the settlements that were reached, and the ongoing impact of these actions.

The Class-Action Lawsuit

In 1973, following the termination of the study, a class-action lawsuit was filed on behalf of the study's participants and their families. The lawsuit accused the U.S. government, the Public Health Service, and other institutions involved in the study of negligence, fraud, and violating the participants' civil rights.

The Settlement

The lawsuit resulted in a $10 million out-of-court settlement in 1974. As part of the settlement, the U.S. government agreed to provide lifetime medical benefits and burial services to the study's participants, their wives, and children who were born with congenital syphilis as a result of the study.

While no amount of money could ever truly compensate the victims and their families for the suffering they experienced, the settlement was an important step in acknowledging the wrongs that had been committed and providing some measure of financial support for those affected.

The Apology from the U.S. Government

In addition to the legal settlement, the Tuskegee Syphilis Study prompted a formal apology from the U.S. government. In 1997, President Bill Clinton issued a public apology on behalf of the nation, expressing remorse for the government's role in the study and acknowledging the pain and suffering endured by the participants and their families.

Ongoing Legal and Ethical Debates

The legal actions and settlements related to the Tuskegee Syphilis Study continue to inform discussions about the ethics of medical research and the responsibility of institutions to protect the rights and well-being of research participants. The study serves as a stark reminder of the importance of ethical oversight and the need to hold those in power accountable for their actions.

The Tuskegee Syphilis Study and its legal aftermath highlight the essential role of the legal system in seeking justice for those who have been wronged by powerful institutions. By understanding the history of these legal actions and settlements, we can appreciate the importance of vigilance and advocacy in ensuring that the rights of research participants are always respected and protected.

5 /
the legacy of the tuskegee syphilis study

impact on medical research ethics

THE TUSKEGEE SYPHILIS Study left an indelible mark on the field of medical research ethics, prompting a series of significant reforms aimed at preventing similar ethical violations in the future. In this section, we'll discuss how the study influenced the development of ethical guidelines, the establishment of oversight bodies, and the overall approach to conducting research involving human subjects.

The Belmont Report and Ethical Principles

One of the most significant outcomes of the Tuskegee Syphilis Study was the creation of the Belmont Report in 1979. This report, developed by the National Commission for the Protection of

Human Subjects of Biomedical and Behavioral Research, outlined three key ethical principles to guide research involving human subjects: respect for persons, beneficence, and justice. These principles form the foundation of modern research ethics and have had a profound impact on the way studies are designed and conducted.

Institutional Review Boards

Another important development in the wake of the Tuskegee Syphilis Study was the establishment of Institutional Review Boards (IRBs). These independent committees, now required for any federally-funded research involving human subjects, are responsible for reviewing research proposals to ensure they adhere to ethical guidelines and protect the rights and welfare of participants. IRBs play a crucial role in preventing unethical research practices and promoting transparency in the research process.

Informed Consent

The Tuskegee Syphilis Study underscored the importance of informed consent in medical research. As a result, researchers are now required to obtain informed consent from participants before they can be included in a study. This process involves providing potential participants with clear, understandable information about the study's purpose, procedures, risks, and benefits, as well as their right to withdraw from the study at any time without penalty. Informed consent is a fundamental aspect of ethical research and helps ensure that participants are treated with dignity and respect.

Focus on Vulnerable Populations

The study's exploitation of a marginalized and economically disadvantaged population highlighted the need to pay special attention to vulnerable groups in research. Today, ethical guidelines emphasize the importance of protecting vulnerable populations, such as children, pregnant women, prisoners, and individuals with cognitive impairments, from potential harm or exploitation in research.

A Lasting Legacy

The impact of the Tuskegee Syphilis Study on medical research ethics cannot be overstated. The study served as a painful reminder of the potential for abuse and exploitation in research and the crucial role of ethical oversight in ensuring the rights and welfare of participants are protected. The lessons learned from this dark chapter in history continue to inform the way research is conducted today, shaping policy, practice, and the education of future generations of researchers.

By understanding the impact of the Tuskegee Syphilis Study on medical research ethics, we can better appreciate the importance of maintaining high ethical standards in research and ensuring that the rights and well-being of all participants are always prioritized.

the ongoing fight for racial equality in healthcare

The Tuskegee Syphilis Study is a stark reminder of the historical mistreatment of African Americans in healthcare and the persistent disparities that continue to exist today. In this section, we'll discuss the ongoing struggle for racial equality in healthcare and the efforts being made to address these disparities and promote equitable access to care for all.

Recognizing Health Disparities

One of the first steps in addressing racial inequality in healthcare is acknowledging the existence of disparities. Research has shown that racial and ethnic minorities often experience poorer health outcomes, lower access to care, and higher rates of chronic illness compared to their white counterparts. These disparities can be attributed to a range of factors, including socioeconomic status, environmental exposures, and systemic biases within the healthcare system.

Culturally Competent Care

A key aspect of promoting racial equality in healthcare is ensuring that medical professionals are trained to provide culturally competent care. This involves developing an understanding of the unique cultural, social, and historical factors that influence the health and well-being of different racial and ethnic groups. By fostering cultural competence, healthcare providers can better meet the needs of diverse populations and work to reduce health disparities.

Addressing Implicit Bias

Implicit biases can influence the way healthcare providers interact with patients and contribute to disparities in care. Recognizing and addressing these biases is crucial in promoting equitable healthcare. Many medical schools and healthcare institutions now incorporate training on implicit bias and its impact on patient care, helping providers become more aware of their own biases and develop strategies to mitigate their effects.

Community Engagement and Advocacy

Engaging with communities and promoting advocacy for racial equality in healthcare is an essential part of the ongoing fight for justice. By partnering with community organizations, healthcare providers, and policymakers, we can work together to identify and address the root causes of health disparities and promote policies that ensure equal access to care for all.

Continuing the Conversation

The legacy of the Tuskegee Syphilis Study serves as a powerful reminder of the importance of maintaining a dialogue about racial inequality in healthcare. By continuing to discuss these issues, we can raise awareness, challenge misconceptions, and drive meaningful change in the way healthcare is delivered and experienced by all individuals, regardless of their race or ethnicity.

The ongoing fight for racial equality in healthcare is a multifaceted and complex issue that requires dedication, collaboration, and a willingness to confront difficult truths. By learning from the past and working together, we can create a more just and equitable healthcare system that meets the needs of all individuals, regardless of their background or circumstances.

commemoration and remembrance

Honoring the memory of the Tuskegee Syphilis Study participants and acknowledging the lasting impact of the study is essential for promoting healing and ensuring that history does not repeat itself. In this section, we'll explore the ways in which the study has been commemorated and remembered, both through official recognition and community-led initiatives.

The Tuskegee Human and Civil Rights Multicultural Center

Established in Tuskegee, Alabama, the Tuskegee Human and Civil Rights Multicultural Center is a museum and educational institution dedicated to preserving the history and legacy of the Tuskegee Syphilis Study. The center provides a space for visitors to learn about the study, its impact on medical research ethics, and the ongoing struggle for racial equality in healthcare.

The National Bioethics Center

In 1997, the same year President Bill Clinton issued a formal apology for the Tuskegee Syphilis Study, the National Center for Bioethics in Research and Health Care was established at Tuskegee University. This center is dedicated to the study and promotion of ethical principles in research and healthcare, with a particular focus on addressing health disparities and promoting racial and ethnic equity.

Annual Commemoration Events

To honor the memory of the study's participants and their families, annual commemoration events are held in Tuskegee and other communities across the United States. These events often include educational programs, panel discussions, and artistic performances, providing an opportunity for reflection and dialogue about the study's lasting impact on medical research ethics and racial equality in healthcare.

Artistic Responses and Cultural Representation

The Tuskegee Syphilis Study has inspired numerous artistic and cultural responses, including plays, novels, documentaries, and visual art. These works serve as a powerful means of engaging with the study's history and raising awareness about its legacy. Through artistic expression, we can promote a deeper understanding of the ethical issues surrounding the study and foster empathy for those who were affected by it.

Teaching Future Generations

Educating future generations about the Tuskegee Syphilis Study is essential for promoting ethical research practices and preventing similar ethical violations in the future. By incorporating the study's history into medical school curricula, bioethics courses, and public education, we can ensure that the lessons learned from this dark chapter in history are not forgotten.

Commemorating and remembering the Tuskegee Syphilis Study is a vital part of acknowledging the suffering endured by its participants and their families, and of promoting healing and growth within the affected communities. By honoring the memory of those who were subjected to this unethical research and reflecting on its broader implications, we can work together to create a more just and ethical healthcare system for all.

conclusion

reflection on the lessons learned from the tuskegee syphilis study

As we reflect on the history and impact of the Tuskegee Syphilis Study, it's important to consider the lessons we can learn from this tragic episode in medical research. By acknowledging and understanding the mistakes of the past, we can work to ensure a more ethical and just future for healthcare and research involving human subjects.

The Importance of Ethical Oversight

The Tuskegee Syphilis Study serves as a powerful reminder of the need for strong ethical oversight in medical research. The establishment of guidelines, such as those outlined in the Belmont Report, and the creation of Institutional Review Boards have been essential in preventing similar ethical violations and promoting the responsible conduct of research.

The Value of Informed Consent

One of the most significant lessons from the study is the importance of informed consent in research involving human subjects. Ensuring that participants are fully informed about the risks and benefits of a study, and that they are able to make an informed decision about their participation, is a fundamental aspect of ethical research.

The Need to Address Health Disparities and Promote Racial Equality

The Tuskegee Syphilis Study highlights the persistent issue of health disparities and the need to address racial inequalities within the healthcare system. By working to promote equitable access to care, culturally competent healthcare, and community engagement, we can help to ensure that all individuals have the opportunity to achieve optimal health and well-being.

The Power of Whistleblowers and Public Advocacy

The role of whistleblowers and public advocates in exposing the Tuskegee Syphilis Study and demanding accountability cannot be understated. Their actions serve as a reminder of the importance of vigilance and advocacy in holding institutions and individuals responsible for their actions, especially when it comes to the protection of vulnerable populations.

The Responsibility of Researchers and Healthcare Professionals

Finally, the study underscores the immense responsibility that researchers and healthcare professionals have to protect the rights and well-being of their research participants and patients. By committing to ethical practices, maintaining transparency, and always putting the needs of the individuals they serve first, these professionals can work to prevent the mistakes of the past from being repeated.

As we reflect on the lessons learned from the Tuskegee Syphilis Study, we must remember that it is up to each of us to carry these lessons forward and work towards a more ethical, just, and equitable future for medical research and healthcare. By understanding the mistakes of the past and committing to a higher standard of ethics, we can create a better world for all.

the importance of continued vigilance in medical ethics and social justice

The Tuskegee Syphilis Study is a stark reminder of the need for ongoing vigilance in upholding medical ethics and advocating for social justice in healthcare. As we work to create a more equitable healthcare system and ensure ethical research practices, we must remain attentive to the issues that persist and continue to engage in proactive efforts to effect change.

Recognizing Emerging Ethical Challenges

In a rapidly evolving medical landscape, it's essential to remain aware of emerging ethical challenges. Advancements in areas like genetics, personalized medicine, and artificial intelligence have the potential to revolutionize healthcare but also pose new ethical concerns. By staying informed and engaged in discussions around these issues, we can help shape the ethical framework that guides the responsible development and application of new medical technologies.

Advocating for Systemic Change

The fight for social justice in healthcare extends beyond the realm of medical ethics and into the broader context of social and economic disparities. Advocating for systemic change, such as addressing socioeconomic barriers to healthcare access and tackling environmental injustices that disproportionately affect marginalized communities, is a crucial part of promoting health equity.

Encouraging Transparency and Accountability

A key lesson from the Tuskegee Syphilis Study is the importance of transparency and accountability in medical research and healthcare. Encouraging open dialogue about research practices, pushing for the regular review of ethical guidelines, and holding institutions accountable for their actions are all essential components of maintaining an ethical and just healthcare system.

Empowering Communities and Individuals

Empowering communities and individuals to advocate for their own health and well-being is an important aspect of continued vigilance in medical ethics and social justice. By promoting health literacy, fostering community engagement, and supporting patient advocacy, we can help ensure that all individuals have the tools and resources they need to make informed decisions about their healthcare and to demand equitable treatment.

Nurturing a Culture of Ethical Responsibility

Finally, it's crucial to cultivate a culture of ethical responsibility among healthcare professionals, researchers, and policymakers. By emphasizing the importance of ethics in medical education and fostering a commitment to ethical practice among all involved in the healthcare system, we can create an environment in which the lessons of the past inform a more just and compassionate future.

The importance of continued vigilance in medical ethics and social justice cannot be overstated. As we work to create a more equitable healthcare system and uphold the highest ethical standards in research and practice, we must remain dedicated to learning from the past, advocating for change, and ensuring that the rights and well-being of all individuals are always at the forefront of our efforts.